Wonders of the World

Written by Cathy Jones
Reading consultants: Christopher Collier and Alan Howe,
Bath Spa University, UK

First published by Parragon in 2009
Parragon
Queen Street House
4 Queen Street
Bath BA1 1HE, UK

ISBN 978-1-4075-8860-5

Printed in China

Wonders of the World

LIVE. LEARN. DISCOVER.

Bath New York Singapore Hong Kong Cologne Delhi Melbourne

Parents' notes

This book is part of a series of nonfiction books designed to appeal to children learning to read.

Each book has been developed with the help of educational experts.

At the end of each book is a quiz to help your child remember the information and the meanings of some of the words and sentences. There is also a glossary of difficult words relating to the subject matter in the book, and an index.

Contents

The Grand Canyon

The Grand Canyon is the biggest **canyon** on the earth. It is a deep valley with steep sides. The Colorado River flows through it.

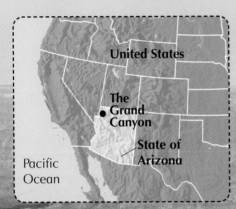

United States

The Grand Canyon

State of Arizona

Pacific Ocean

The Grand Canyon is 5,250 feet deep, 277 miles long, and up to 19 miles wide.

The Colorado River has worn through layers of rock. The oldest rocks at the bottom are almost 2 billion years old.

You can look down at the canyon through the glass floor of the Skywalk. The Skywalk juts over the canyon 4,000 feet above the river.

Grand Canyon

Heavy summer rain, winter storms, and melting snow flow into the Colorado River as waterfalls.

Niagara Falls

Niagara Falls lies between the U.S. and Canada. The Niagara River flows around three **islands** and splits into three waterfalls. These are the Horseshoe Falls, American Falls, and Bridal Veil Falls.

NORTH AMERICA

Niagara Falls

A waterfall is made when a river flows over layers of rock and over time wears away the soft rock. A shelf of hard rock is left for the water to fall over.

Niagara Falls

In 1901, a 63-year-old schoolteacher named Annie Edson Taylor became the first person to go over Niagara Falls in a wooden barrel—and live to tell the tale!

At night, most of Niagara's water flows through tunnels to make electricity.

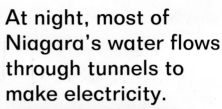

About 100,000 cubic feet of water thunder over the falls every second. That's about the same amount of water as in a large swimming pool.

waterfalls

The Sahara

Sahara

The Sahara is the world's biggest hot **desert**. It covers most of northern Africa. It is one of the hottest and driest places on earth. Very few plants and animals can live here.

Camels are desert animals. The camel stores fat in its hump. It can live on the fat when it has no food or water.

An oasis is a pool of water in the desert. The water comes from deep under the ground. Plants and trees grow around it.

One of the most deadly scorpions in the world lives in the Sahara. The fat-tailed scorpion has a poisonous sting in its tail. It hides from the desert sun under stones or logs.

Western Sahara

Algeria

Libya

Egypt

Mauritania

Sahara

Mali

Niger

Chad

Sudan

Ethiopia

AFRICA

The Great Barrier Reef

The Great Barrier Reef is the largest living thing in the world. It is made up of tiny animals called coral polyps. Millions of these animals have joined together to make a **reef** that runs for over 1,200 miles.

Coral polyps are tiny sea animals that make their own skeletons of stone. Over hundreds of years, the skeletons build into coral reefs.

Indian Ocean

The Great Barrier Reef

AUSTRALIA

Indian Ocean

Coral reefs are home to thousands of other animals, from tiny clown fish to big green turtle s.

Great Barrier Reef

The Great Barrier Reef is the only living thing that can be seen from outer space.

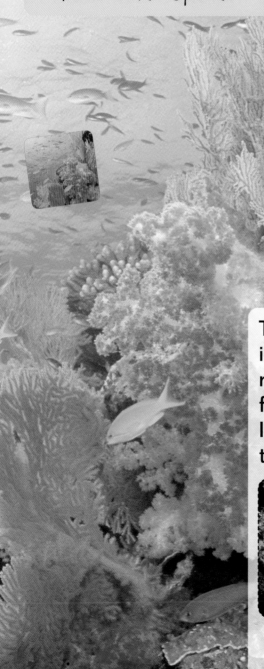

The giant clam sticks itself to a spot on the reef and stays there for the rest of its life. Its shell can grow to 4 feet.

The Amazon rain forest

The Amazon **rain forest** is the biggest in the world. It covers an area the size of Australia. Over 180 inches of rain can fall in a year.

The Amazon River begins in the Andes Mountains in Peru and flows through Brazil into the Atlantic Ocean.

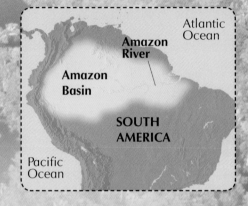

Atlantic Ocean

Amazon River

Amazon Basin

SOUTH AMERICA

Pacific Ocean

jaguar

The jaguar is one of the biggest **predators** in the Amazon rain forest.

... tallest trees grow up to 130 feet tall. Their branches make a leafy blanket called the canopy. Brightly colored macaws, toucans, and parrots live here.

Amazon rain forest

The anaconda snake spends a lot of its time in the water.

The Pyramids of Giza

The three great **pyramids** at Giza are over 4,500 years old. They were built for the **pharaohs** Khufu, his son Khafre, and his grandson Menkaure. These massive tombs were burial chambers, although no one has ever found a **mummy** inside them.

The base of the Great Pyramid is an almost perfect square.

The Sphinx guards the way to Khafre's pyramid. It has the head of the king and the body of a lion.

16

earth Skywalk oasis

camel scorpion clown fish

giant clam

anaconda toucan macaws

druids pyramids

gladiator parrot

watchtower Sphinx

Over two million blocks of stone were needed to build Khufu's Great Pyramid.

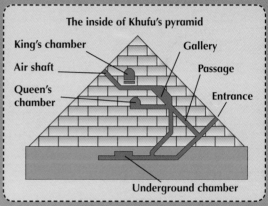

The inside of Khufu's pyramid

King's chamber

Gallery

Air shaft

Passage

Queen's chamber

Entrance

Underground chamber

Stonehenge

No one knows why this huge stone circle was built. It was probably built about 4,500 years ago at the end of the Stone Age. It may have been a temple where Celtic druids worshipped nature.

Pairs of stones, joined by a lintel, stand in two circles, one inside the other. The stones stand on a **henge**—a high bank circled by a ditch.

lintel

sarsen stone

Stonehenge

Druids still gather at Stonehenge every year on Midsummer's Day to watch the sun rise.

Some **archaeologists** think that Stonehenge was used to measure the movements of the sun and moon.

Atlantic
Ocean

**United
Kingdom**

●Stonehenge

The Great Wall of China

The Great Wall of China is the longest man-made object in the world. It winds for more than 3,700 miles through mountains, deserts, and **marshes**.

Over 2,000 years ago, Emperor Qin Shi Huangdi built the wall to stop enemies from invading from the north.

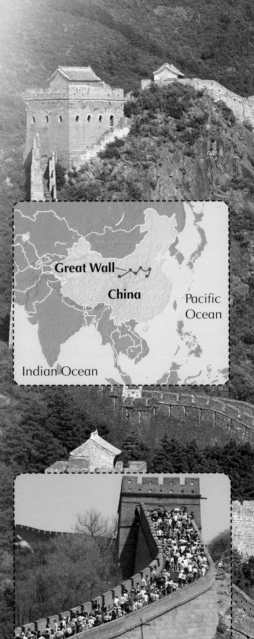

Great Wall

China

Pacific Ocean

Indian Ocean

The wall was wide enough for ten soldiers to march side by side.

Watchtowers were built all along the wall. Guards sent messages to the next watchtower using smoke signals.

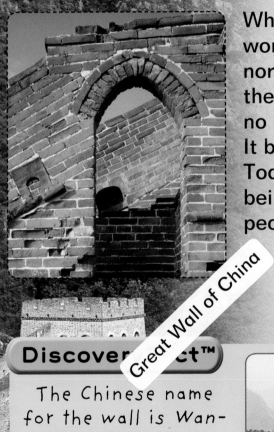

When the Chinese won the land in the north 350 years ago, the Great Wall was no longer needed. It began to fall down. Today, the wall is being fixed for people to enjoy.

Great Wall of China

Discover Fact™

The Chinese name for the wall is Wan-Li Wang-Qeng. It means 10,000-Li-Long-Wall (10,000 Li is about 3,000 miles).

The Colosseum

This open-air **amphitheater** in Rome was built in Roman times. Crowds packed the Colosseum to watch plays, mock sea battles, and **gladiator** fights.

Colosseum

Inside the circular building, rows of seats are arranged in tiers. A crowd of 50,000 people would all have a good view of the action.

EUROPE

Italy

Rome

Mediterranean Sea

Animals and fighters waited in rooms and tunnels beneath the arena for their turn to fight.

Gladiators were usually slaves or criminals who were trained to fight each other, or wild animals, to the death.

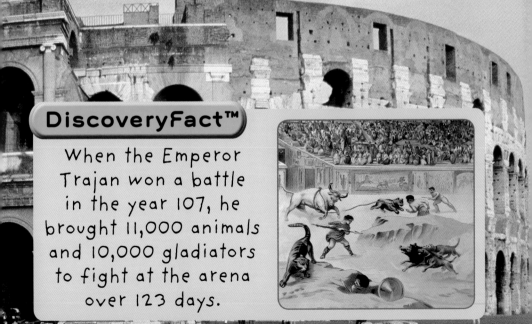

DiscoveryFact™

When the Emperor Trajan won a battle in the year 107, he brought 11,000 animals and 10,000 gladiators to fight at the arena over 123 days.

New York City

New York City has one of the most famous skylines in the world. It is made up of skyscrapers such as The Empire State Building and the Chrysler Building.

New York City is built on islands, including Manhattan and Staten Island. Part of it is also on the mainland.

This picture shows skyscrapers on Manhattan.

New York City

New York State

New York City

United States

Atlantic Ocean

Pacific Ocean

The Statue of Liberty was a gift from France in 1886 to mark 100 years of American independence.

New York is called the Big Apple. It was given its nickname by jazz musicians in the 1930s.

Central Park k in Manhattan has a lake, a zoo, a theater, and an outdoor ice rink.

Times Square is famous for its electric advertising billboards and theaters.

Quiz

Now try this quiz!

All the answers can be found in this book.

How many soldiers could march side by side along the Great Wall of China?

(a) Three
(b) Five
(c) Ten

What is New York's nickname?

(a) Big Apple
(b) Big Orange
(c) Big Peach

Where does the Amazon River start?

(a) The Atlas Mountains
(b) The Andes Mountains
(c) The Rocky Mountains

What statue guards the entrance to Khafre's pyramid?

(a) Mermaid
(b) Centaur
(c) Sphinx

Where is the Sahara?

(a) Africa
(b) Australia
(c) South America

Which Roman emperor won a battle in the year 107?

(a) Julius Caesar
(b) Trajan
(c) Hadrian

Glossary

Archaeologist Someone who studies ancient remains to make sense of the past.

Amphitheater A circular theater with tiers of seating for the crowd surrounding an arena at the center.

Canyon A narrow, steep-sided valley, usually with a river at the bottom.

Desert A dry, hot place where few plants and animals live.

Gladiator A fighter in ancient Rome trained to fight other gladiators or wild animals to the death.

Henge An ancient large, raised, circular mound of earth, which is flat on top and surrounded by a ditch.

Island An area of land surrounded by water.

Marsh   An area of wet land.

Mummy   A dead body that has been preserved and wrapped in cloth.

Predator   An animal that hunts another animal for food.

Pyramid   An ancient stone tomb with a square base and four triangular sides that reach a point at the top.

Pharaoh   An ancient Egyptian ruler.

Rain forest   An area of forest that has a lot of rainfall and usually high temperatures.

Reef   A raised area of coral, rock, or sand just below the surface of the ocean.

Index

mummy 16

n
New York City 24–25
Niagara Falls 8–9
Niagara River 8

o
oasis 11

p
parrots 15
pharaohs 16
Pyramids 16–17

r
rain forests 14–15
rocks 6, 8
Romans 22–23

s
Sahara 10–11
scorpions 11
skyscrapers 24
Skywalk 7
snakes 15
South America 14–15
Sphinx 16
Statue of Liberty 25
stone circles 18–19
Stonehenge 18–19

t
Taylor, Annie Edson 9
temperatures 7
Times Square 25
toucans 15
Trajan, Emperor 19
turtles 12

u
United Kingdom 18–19
United States 6–7, 8–9,
    24–25

w
watchtowers 21
waterfalls 7, 8–9

Acknowledgments

t=top, c=center, b=bottom, r=right, l=left

Front cover: Getty Images/Robert Francis
Back cover: l Getty Images, r Getty Images

Corbis
1, 2, 3, 5t, 5bl, 5br, 6-7, 6b, 7tr, 7tl, 7b, 10-11, 11r, 12b, 14, 15t,
15b, 18-19, 18l, 18r, 19t, 20-21, 20, 21t, 21c, 22-23, 23c, 24-25, 25tl,
25bl, 25br

Getty Images
4, 14-15, 16-17, 16, 21b, 23b, 25tr,

istockphoto
8-9, 9t, 9b

Digital Vision
12-13

NASA
13t